MANGROVES
GROW IN SALT WATER!

By Janey Levy

Gareth Stevens
PUBLISHING

Please visit our website, www.garethstevens.com. For a free color catalog of all our high-quality books, call toll free 1-800-542-2595 or fax 1-877-542-2596.

Library of Congress Cataloging-in-Publication Data

Names: Levy, Janey, author.
Title: Mangroves grow in salt water! / Janey Levy.
Description: New York : Gareth Stevens Publishing, [2020] | Series: World's
   weirdest plants | Includes index.
Identifiers: LCCN 2019030741 | ISBN 9781538246474 | ISBN 9781538246481
   (library binding) | ISBN 9781538246467 (paperback) | ISBN 9781538246498
   (ebook)
Subjects: LCSH: Rhizophoraceae–Juvenile literature.
Classification: LCC QK495.R46 L48 2020 | DDC 583/.69–dc23
LC record available at https://lccn.loc.gov/2019030741

First Edition

Published in 2020 by
Gareth Stevens Publishing
111 East 14th Street, Suite 349
New York, NY 10003

Copyright © 2020 Gareth Stevens Publishing

Designer: Katelyn E. Reynolds
Editor: Abby Badach Doyle

Photo credits: Cover, p. 1 PixHound/Shutterstock.com; cover, pp. 1–24 (background) Conny Sjostrom/
Shutterstock.com; cover, pp. 1–24 (sign elements) A Sk/Shutterstock.com; p. 5 Mazur Travel/Shutterstock.com;
p. 7 Andrei Minsk/Shutterstock.com; pp. 9, 11 (propagules) Ekaterina Malskaya/Shutterstock.com; p. 11
(mangrove graphic) Supawadee/Shutterstock.com; p. 11 (leaves) socrates471/Shutterstock.com; p. 11
(branches) AJP/Shutterstock.com; p. 11 (trunk) ben bryant /Shutterstock.com; p. 11 (prop roots) Ilan
Ejzykowicz/Shutterstock.com; p. 13 Joost van Uffelen/Shutterstock.com; p. 15 Damsea/Shutterstock.com;
p. 17 Education Images/Universal Images Group via GettyImages; p. 19 (main) Wahyu Adji Febrianto/
Shutterstock.com; p. 19 (inset) nirapai boonpheng/Shutterstock.com; p. 21 Lekko17/Shutterstock.com.

Printed in the United States of America

Some of the images in this book illustrate individuals who are models. The depictions do not imply actual
situations or events.

CPSIA compliance information: Batch #CW20GS : For further information contact Gareth Stevens, New York, New York at 1-800-542-2595.

CONTENTS

Words in the glossary appear in **bold** type
the first time they are used in the text.

MEET THE MANGROVE

You know what a tree looks like, right? It has roots under the ground, and above the ground, it has a **trunk**, branches, leaves, flowers, and fruit. Well, the mangrove doesn't look quite like other trees.

The mangrove is one weird tree. It has the usual trunk, branches, leaves, flowers, and fruit. But its roots are above the ground. And unlike other trees, it's able to grow in salt water! Inside this book, you'll discover lots more about this strange tree.

SEEDS OF KNOWLEDGE

Many kinds of mangroves exist. In the Americas, the main kind of mangrove is the common, or red, mangrove.

The name "mangrove" is also used for the forests made up of mangrove trees.

5

MANGROVE HOME AND HABITAT

Where can you find mangroves? They don't like cold, so they live in and near the **tropics**. They grow in Southeast Asia, India, Australia, New Zealand, Africa, and the Americas.

In the countries where they live, mangroves grow along the coasts. There, the water and soil are salty. There's also not much **oxygen** in the soil, but the trees do need some oxygen to survive. These conditions would kill most plants. But as you'll discover, mangroves have surprising **adaptations** that help them succeed.

SEEDS OF KNOWLEDGE

About 80 species, or kinds, of mangroves exist. Only 12 species are found in the Americas.

WHERE MANGROVES LIVE

NORTH
AMERICA

ATLANTIC
OCEAN

EUROPE

ASIA

PACIFIC
OCEAN

AFRICA

SOUTH
AMERICA

PACIFIC
OCEAN

INDIAN
OCEAN

AUSTRALIA

☐ mangroves

This shows the places in the world where you can find mangroves.

IT STARTS AS A SEED

You likely know many trees grow from seeds that have fallen to the ground or been planted. Mangroves grow from seeds but not in the usual way.

After mangrove flowers are **pollinated**, the tree produces fruit with seeds. These start immediately growing into baby trees, called propagules (PRAH-puh-gyoolz), while they're still on the parent tree! They may fall into the mud below the parent and grow there. Or they may be carried away on the ocean and take root somewhere else. That's pretty weird!

In propagules, a long root comes out of the seed and grows downward.

9

NOT LIKE OTHER TREES

As you read earlier, mangroves have the usual trunk, branches, leaves, flowers, and fruit. But their roots are quite strange looking.

Red mangroves have **prop** roots that grow in a tangle above the ground. The prop roots grow outward from the trunk and curve down to reach the soil. Black mangroves have roots that grow outward under the ground. But along these roots are roots that shoot straight up above the ground. The mangrove has good reasons for growing these weird roots!

SEEDS OF KNOWLEDGE

The roots of the black mangrove that stick straight up above the ground are called pneumatophores (nyoo-MAA-tuh-fohrz).

The Mangrove Tree

leaves

branches

propagules

trunk

prop roots

Here are the parts of the mangrove tree. What looks the same from trees you have seen? What looks different?

TANGLED ROOTS

Mangroves have roots above the ground for a reason. The trees need oxygen to survive, and the soil where they grow lacks it. So their special roots have openings called lenticels (LEHN-tuh-sehlz) that take oxygen from the air!

Those roots can do something even more surprising. Like all plants, mangroves need fresh water, even though they grow in salt water. So, for many types of mangroves, the roots actually make fresh water. How? They keep the salt in the ocean water from ever entering the plant. Wow!

SEEDS OF KNOWLEDGE

While some mangroves don't allow salt to enter at all, others deal with salt a different way. They allow salt to enter, but then get rid of it through their leaves.

Because mangroves have adaptations to deal with salt, they can live in water that's up to 100 times saltier than most other plants can stand!

13

CREATURES BIG AND SMALL

These special mangrove trees create beautiful **ecosystems**. All sorts of creatures depend on mangroves for food or cover. Crabs and bugs eat the leaves. **Fungi** eat rotting matter from the trees.

Birds such as pelicans and roseate spoonbills nest among mangroves. Saltwater crocodiles, bats known as flying foxes, and monkeys live in mangroves. **Manatees**, monitor lizards, and sea turtles find shelter among mangroves. Mangroves provide **nursery** areas for many kinds of fish. Without mangroves, these and many other creatures would suffer.

SEEDS OF KNOWLEDGE

Some uncommon animals depend on mangroves. These include pygmy three-toed sloths, mangrove hummingbirds, rainbow parrotfish, and fish called Goliath groupers.

Underwater, ocean creatures such as sponges, snails, worms, anemones, and barnacles hang onto the roots of the mangroves.

15

ADDITIONAL MANGROVE ADVANTAGES

Mangroves provide many benefits to people as well. People get wood that they can burn or use for building. Other parts of the trees can be used for dyes, soap, makeup, food, and **medicine**.

Mangroves also help keep coasts safe from wind and waves, especially during storms. The roots trap sand, dirt, and other matter, which keeps the water cleaner. Mangroves also help fight **climate change** by lowering the amount of the gas carbon dioxide in the air. They do this by storing carbon.

SEEDS OF KNOWLEDGE

One acre (0.4 ha) of mangrove forest can store 1,450 pounds (658 kg) of carbon. That's about how much carbon is given off by one car driving across the US three times!

16

A mangrove forest can reduce the harmful power of a tsunami (soo-NAH-me), or giant ocean wave, by as much as 90 percent.

17

ENEMIES TO MANGROVES

Sadly, these important trees are in danger. Every year between 2001 and 2012, from 35 to 97 square miles (91 to 251 sq km) of mangrove forest disappeared.

There are several reasons for what's happening to mangrove forests. People are building homes and businesses along coasts. As climate change increases, sea levels are rising and hurting mangroves. But the biggest problem is shrimp farming. People are cutting down mangrove forests so they can put shrimp farms where the forests used to be.

SEEDS OF KNOWLEDGE

Pollution is also harming mangrove forests. The pollution comes from oil spills and from matter used on farms that washes down to the coasts.

People are building lots of shrimp farms because people in the United States, Europe, Japan, and China are eating more shrimp.

shrimp

19

SAVING MANGROVES

Even though mangroves are in danger, there is good news. People have realized how important mangroves are to human communities and ecosystems around the world. So they're taking steps to save them.

Governments are putting laws in place to keep mangroves safe and renew mangrove forests that have been lost. In 1986, a man named Robin Lewis figured out the best way to replant mangrove forests. His method is now used around the world. The work of saving mangroves isn't finished, but now there's hope.

SEEDS OF KNOWLEDGE

Groups such as the Mangrove Alliance, World Wide Fund for Nature, and Mangroves for the Future are working to help bring back mangrove forests around the world.

20

Robin Lewis learned that baby mangrove trees grow best when they are dry 70 percent of the time and wet for 30 percent of the time.

21

GLOSSARY

adaptation: a change in a type of plant or animal that makes it better able to live in its surroundings

climate change: long-term change in Earth's climate, caused partly by human activities such as burning oil and natural gas

ecosystem: all the living things in an area

fungus: a living thing that is somewhat like a plant, but doesn't make its own food, have leaves, or have a green color. Fungi include molds and mushrooms.

manatee: a large animal that lives in warm waters and eats plants

medicine: a drug taken to make a sick person well

nursery: a place where young animals can grow and are cared for

oxygen: a colorless, odorless gas that many animals, including people, need to breathe

pollinate: to take pollen from one flower, plant, or tree to another

prop: something that is used to support something and keep it in place

tropics: the warm parts of Earth near the equator

trunk: the thick main stem of a tree

FOR MORE INFORMATION

Books

Bow, James. *Forests Inside Out.* New York, NY: Crabtree Publishing Co., 2015.

Burnie, David. *Seashore.* New York, NY: DK Children, 2017.

Colozza Cocca, Lisa. *Estuary Animals.* Greensboro, NC: Carson-Dellosa, 2019.

Websites

Mangrove Ecology
mangroveactionproject.org/mangrove-ecology/
Learn more about mangroves on this website.

Mangroves: Photos of Plants and Animals
ocean.si.edu/ocean-life/plants-algae/mangroves-photos-plants-and-animals
Discover more about mangroves on this site and see some great photos.

INDEX